Numbers For Kids

Donald Simpson

Copyright © 2019 by Donald Simpson

All rights Reserved. No part of this publication or the information in it may be quoted from or reproduced in any form by means such as printing, scanning, photocopying or otherwise without prior written permission of the copyright holder.

ONE

TWO

FOUR

FIVE

SIX

SEVEN

EIGHT

NINE

ELEVEN

TWELVE

THIRTEEN

FOURTEEN

SIXTEEN

SEVENTEEN

EIGHTEEN

NINETEEN

TWENTY

TWENTY ONE

TWENTY TWO

TWENTY THREE

TWENTY FOUR

TWENTY SIX

TWENTY SEVEN

TWENTY EIGHT

TWENTY NINE

THIRTY

CPSIA information can be obtained
at www.ICGtesting.com
Printed in the USA
LVHW071040221119
R15400900005B/R154009PG637665LVX34B/3/P